PENGUIN DREAMS
AND STRANGER THINGS

Bloom County books by Berke Breathed

LOOSE TAILS
'TOONS FOR OUR TIMES
PENGUIN DREAMS and Stranger Things

C

LIBRARY OF CONGRESS CATALOG CARD NUMBER 85-40012

Published simultaneously in Canada
by Little, Brown & Company (Canada) Limited

PRINTED IN THE UNITED STATES OF AMERICA

MILO'S ALBUM

A Personal Photographic Statement

A self portrait. Behind is
the boarding house. Steve
Dallas' room is in the back.
(250 at f/6)

A private moment. Steve Dallas sings Julio Iglesias. I was under the bed.

The USS Starchair "Enterpoop" slips into Warp Drive. Mr. Spock watches for "The Wild Planet of Open-minded Stewardesses"

Oliver Wendell Jones disciplines a
reluctant Banana Junior Computer,
apparently eager to catch "2010"
at the Bijou

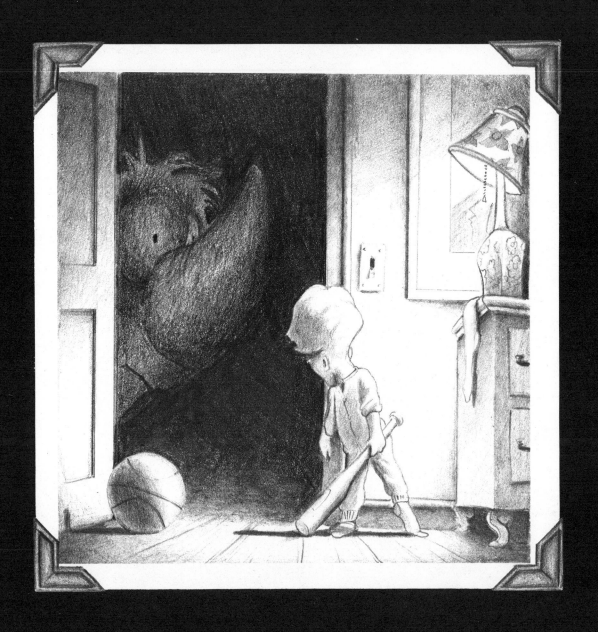

*Binkley finally confronts his neuroses
in the only appropriate manner.*

November 5, 1984...
A gallant sense of optimism
prevails in the face of
impending, overwhelming
stomach-churning
political catastrophe.

"But the calculations were
Correct!"
The scientific pursuit of the
first long-tailed hamster
is dealt yet another serious
blow.

7:13 a.m., Sunday morning.
"Quality Time"

11

WELL...I MUST SAY...THIS CRUISE HASN'T EXACTLY BEEN WHAT I EXPECTED. AT LEAST I CAN LOOK FORWARD TO A GOOD GOURMET DIN—....

UH...WHAT'S THIS?

BEAN CURD AND SHREDDED WHEAT.

OH. ACTUALLY I WAS HOPING FOR A NICE BIG STEAK...

MEAT?!?

NO?...UH...WELL, I LOVE SHREDDED WHEAT, TOO! YES...YES, I'LL JUST EAT SCRUMPTIOUS SHREDDED WHEAT. NO PROBLEM.

ANY SUGAR?

REFINED SUGAR?!?

EXCUSE ME, FELLOW SHIPMATES...BUT I WONDER IF YOU MIGHT EXPLAIN JUST WHAT THE DICKENS IS GOING ON AROUND HERE...

THIS CRUISE SEEMS TO BE NOTHING BUT A BUNCH OF BEAN CURD NIBBLERS WALKING AROUND TALKING TO WHALES AND PLANNING "CONFRONTATIONS" WITH NUKE WASTE DUMPERS. NOW, JUST WHAT IS ALL... UH... ALL...

...GOOD HEAVENS!... OF COURSE! WHY,...YOU ALL ARE...ARE...

ENVIRONMENTAL EXTREMISTS.!!

NO! YES!

T WAS THE DAY BEFORE CHRISTMAS, AND FAR OUT AT SEA, A PENGUIN WAS SEARCHING FOR HIS MOM, PATIENTLY.

FOR, YOU SEE, ONE CAN MANAGE GROUNDHOG DAY WITHOUT HOGS... BUT A CHRISTMAS LESS MOTHERS IS STRICTLY FOR THE DOGS!

RAINBOW WARRIOR

SO WHILE WE ALL SIT, IN OUR HOMES COMFORTABLY, WITH FAMILY ABOUT, CHUGGING EGGNOG AND TEA...

RAINBOW WARRIOR

...LET'S REMEMBER ALL THOSE ON TOMORROW'S BRIGHT DAWN, WHO'LL BE CUDDLING THEIR NOSE, IN PLACE OF A MOM...

YEAH!

13

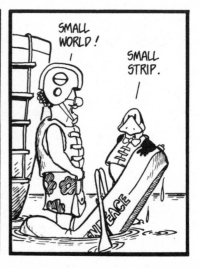

AND SO, HOME. AND WITH AN UNSUCCESSFUL CONCLUSION TO THE ANTARCTIC "MOMQUEST"... THE MOOD JUST ISN'T VERY GOOD...

PHPHPT!

..HIJACKED BY "GREENPEACE"... HARPOONED BY RUSSIAN WHALERS, INVOLUNTARILY RESCUED BY U.S. MARINES...

PHPHPT!

YES, IT IS TIMES LIKE THESE WHEN IT IS BEST FOR ALL CON-CERNED THAT WE BECOME JUST ONE VERY SPECIAL THING...

...ALONE.

PHPHPT!

MY LIFE NEEDS SPIRITUALITY. YEP. THAT'S IT. I NEED RELIGION.

BUT WHICH ONE? I MEAN, THERE'S A LOT RIDING ON THIS.

CHECKED THE "YELLOW PAGES"?

OH, IT'S A CONSUMER'S NIGHTMARE. TOO MANY BRAND NAMES.

I WOULDN'T TAKE ANY CHANCES.

I'M JOINING 'EM ALL.

GOOD EVENING. TODAY'S TOP STORY: GIANT RADIOACTIVE SALAMANDERS ARE MOVING UP FROM MEXICO AND DEVOURING ALL PUDGY, FLIGHTLESS WATERFOWL.

YOU'RE KIDDING!

WE'RE NOT KIDDING.

YOU HAVE TO BE KIDDING!

WE'RE NOT KIDDING.

OH MY GOODNESS... OH MY GOODNESS... YOU'VE GOTTA BE KIDDING!!

WELL, WE'RE KIDDING A LITTLE.

THE MEDIA'S GETTING COCKY!

FOR THOSE NEW VIEWERS OUT THERE, I WOULD HAVE YOU BE AWARE THAT BEHIND ME IS MY CLOSET OF ANXIETIES. OR RATHER, IT USED TO BE MINE.

FOR I AM NOW AN EMOTIONALLY STABLE PERSON. COMPLETELY. AND ANXIETIES HAVE NO INTEREST IN WELL-ADJUSTED PERSONALITIES... UNLIKE, I'M AFRAID, MOST OF YOURS.

KNOCK! KNOCK!

IN SHORT, ASK NOT FOR WHOM THE CLOSET KNOCKS... IT KNOCKS FOR THEE, NOT ME!

BINKLEY! OH, BINKLEY! WE HAVE A FULL MENU OF ANXIETIES TONIGHT!! PLEASE CHOOSE THE NIGHTMARE OF YOUR CHOICE FROM THE FOLLOWING:

A: JESSE HELMS EXPLAINING AT LENGTH HOW MARTIN LUTHER KING WAS A COMMUNIST.
B: A CONVENTION OF "PM MAGAZINE" HOSTS.
C: A HUGE, BINKLEY-EATING PYTHON.

I'LL TAKE THE PYTHON.

GREAT! I'LL SEND IT RIGHT OUT!

HECK, I'M NO GLUTTON FOR PUNISHMENT.

Y...YOU'RE FROM MY ANXIETY CLOSET?

YES. WE'RE TWO EXPERT ECONOMISTS. WE'LL BE YOUR NIGHTMARE TONIGHT.

TWO ECONOMISTS?! IN THE SAME ROOM? PLEASE... JUST DON'T DISCUSS THE ECONOMY!

THE ECONOMY? OH, IT'S IMPROVING!

NO, IT'S NOT.

GENTLE-MEN...

THE LEADING ECONOMIC INDICATORS SHOW A SUSTAINED RENOBERATION TOWARDS—

PHOOEY! THE DEFICIT! WHAT OF THE DEFICIT!

AAIGH!

THE KEY, OF COURSE, IS THE DEFICIT.

THE DEFICIT, MY FANNY...

HERE, APPARENTLY, ARE A PAIR OF EXPERT "SURVIVALISTS" ON THEIR WAY TO DIG A BOMB SHELTER IN THE MEADOW... SAY, BOYS, ANY TIPS FOR US AMATEURS?...

NO NO... RUSH! RUSH! NO TIME TO CHAT...

WHAT ABOUT FOOD? WHAT DO EXPERT SURVIVALISTS PLAN TO EAT AFTER THE "BIG ONE" DROPS?

EAT? WELL,.. AS I UNDER-STAND IT, WE'LL BE HUNTIN'... MAYBE A LITTLE 'COON... 'POSSUM ...SOME RABBIT...

POING!

NOW JUST WAIT ONE ☆⊙!!?# MINUTE...

DID YA GET ALL THE SUPPLIES?

YESSIR! K-MART WAS OPEN LATE.

LESSEE... 9MM AMMO...WATER PURIFIERS...GAS MASKS... FALLOUT SUITS...RADIATION SICKNESS PILLS...RADIOACTIVITY DETECTORS... UH...

AWRIGHT. HOLD IT...

WHERE'S THE MUTANT REPELLENT?

AW SHOOT...

LET'S SEE, NOW... "CONDUCT A SURVIVALIST DRILL," HE SAID..."THE BOMBS HAVE DROPPED AND YOUR DUTY IS TO DEFEND THE RADIOACTIVE RUBBLE OF THE MIDWEST AGAINST THE ENEMY..."

"...AND ALL YOU'VE GOT IS YOUR GUN...WHICH IS LIKE A MISTRESS; TREAT HER WITH RESPECT AND SHE'LL NEVER POOP OUT ON YOU."

"SO GRASP HER RESPECTFULLY... SIGHT ENEMY... AND SLOWLY SQUEE--"

MY MISTRESS IS POOPED, THE REDS HAVE OKLAHOMA, AND I'M GOING TO BED.

HELLO? **MTV**? WHAT'RE YA TRYIN' TO DO TO MY BOY, NOW? HE SPENDS ALL DAY SPINNING AROUND ON HIS HEAD...

WOOSH! WOOSH! WOOSH!

IT'S CALLED WHAT? "BREAK-DANCING"? WHAT THE HECK IS "BREAKDANCING"? I DON'T THINK I WANT MY SON DOING "BREAK" ANYTHING!

WOOSH! WOOSH! *CRASH!* OUCH!

SON?... SON?...

WELL **NOW** HE'S ★@#* **BROKEN!**

HELLO? COUNTY EMERGENCY? YES, I'VE GOT A GOOF OF A SON HERE WHO CLAIMS TO BE GRAVELY INJURED.

YES... AS I UNDERSTAND IT, HE WAS "BREAKDANCING." RIGHT. "BREAKDANCING." HUH?... WELL, I'LL ASK HIM...

WHAT'D YA BREAK?

MY HEAD.

HIS HEAD. GOT ANY NEW ONES?

THE FOLLOWING SOUND OF A "BOO-BOO BURGER" BEING EATEN IS BROUGHT TO YOU BY YOUR LOCAL "BOO-BOO BURGER" RESTAURANT, OPEN LATE TONIGHT...

OH NO...

MUNCH! MMM! CHOMP OH...MM! SLURP! SMACK!

CHEW... MUNCH! MM! AH... SMACK! LICK! OH...OH YES... CHOMP! SLURP! CHOMP! MUNCH! OH! MM! SLURP!

I ★@#?! **HATE** "BOO-BOO BURGERS."

Boo-Boo Burger

24

YES...WELL, I'M CERTAINLY VERY HAPPY THAT YOU WERE ABLE TO BUY THE BLOOM COUNTY TELEPHONE CO., MR. POODINSKI...

THANKS TO THE FEDS!

YEP! NOTHIN' LIKE A COMPETITIVE MARKET TO KEEP THE CUSTOMERS HAPPY!

UH...SPEAKING OF CUSTOMERS... I WONDER IF I COULD GET A NEW EXTENSION PHONE INSTALLED?

NO SWEAT! WHAT'S A GOOD DAY FOR YA?

UH... TUESDAY.

FINE. HOW'S JULY OF '86?

BARTENDER! I'LL HAVE A CUP OF COFFEE! STRAIGHT UP!

COFFEE LETS YOU CALM YOURSELF DOWN WHILE IT PICKS YOU UP! AND I'M ONE OF THE NEW COFFEE GENERATION!... ONE OF TODAY'S MOVERS AND SHAKERS! YESSIR... I'VE JOINED *THE COFFEE ACHIEVERS!!*

OR IS IT ALL JUST A BUNCH OF HOOEY?

GOOD MORNING, DAD. I BROUGHT YOU SOME MILK AND DOUGHNUTS. YOU'LL NEED THE NOURISHMENT FOR THE TASK AHEAD.

BELOVED FATHER OF MINE... I CAN NOW ANNOUNCE THAT EVERY ONE OF YOUR CIGARETTES HAS BEEN SECURELY HIDDEN. AS WELL AS YOUR CAR KEYS. IN SHORT, THIS WEEKEND WILL BE SPENT SANS TOBACCO.

HAVING SAID THAT, LET'S BEGIN THERAPY. READY?

HERE, OF COURSE, IS AN ENLARGEMENT OF A DISEASED LUNG. IN COLOR.

PTEWPH!

27

THAT'S IT, SON. YOU WIN. I GIVE UP. I'VE TOTALLY AND SHAMEFULLY DEGRADED AND HUMILIATED MYSELF.

SO, NO MORE SMOKING. NOPE! NEVER AGAIN. I'LL PROMISE...

IF...UH...IF YOU'LL JUST TELL ME ONE SILLY, NAGGING, LITTLE THING...

JUST WHERE THE **HECK** DID YOU HIDE MY CIGARET—

TOILET.

I'VE BEEN ASKED BY THE MANAGEMENT TO ANNOUNCE THAT, STARTING TODAY, YET ANOTHER NEWSPAPER WILL BE PRINTING THIS FEATURE...NAMELY, THE **TULSA DAILY HERALD.** SO FAR, THAT MAKES A TOTAL OF SIX NATIONWIDE. OBVIOUSLY, WE'RE VERY EXCITED.

BLOOM TOURS

SO, TO HELP OUR NEW VIEWERS IN TULSA, I THOUGHT IT'D BE NICE TO SPEND THE NEXT FEW WEEKS CONDUCTING A BASIC INTRODUCTORY TOUR OF BLOOM COUNTY.

BLOOM TOURS

YES...WELL...NOW THEN... WE CAN START RIGHT HERE. WE'RE STANDING IN "MILO'S MEADOW." OVER THERE IS "BINKLEY." TO MY LEFT HERE IS "PORTNOY."..

BLOOM TOURS

AND ME? I'M "MICHAEL JACKSON."

MY FANNY.

BLOOM TOURS

AND NOW, FOR THE BENEFIT OF ALL OUR NEW READERS IN TULSA, LET'S FIRST VISIT THE GRAVE- SITE OF BLOOM COUNTY'S MOST FAMOUS AND HIGHLY RESPECTED FORMER RESIDENT...**BILL THE CAT.** HE WAS — HEY! WHAT'S THIS?!

BLOOM TOURS

AHOY, MAN! STOP THAT! WOULD YOU SO EASILY TREAD UPON THE HOLY RESTING PLACE OF LINCOLN? OR KENNEDY? OR ELVIS?!

ZZZ... SNORT!

BILL 1980-1983

SHOO! SCRAM! AWAY WITH YOU, YOU DISRESPECTFUL SCALAWAG!

WAP! WAP! WAP!

BILL

BLOOM TOURS

I'M SO EMBARRASSED! BILL THE CAT IS CONSIDERED A NEAR- DEITY BY EVERYONE! TRULY!

POINK! POINK! POINK!

BILL

BLOOM TOURS

29

AND THIS, FOR OUR NEW FRIENDS READING US IN TULSA, IS WHAT WE ALL CALL "BINKLEY'S CLOSET OF ANXIETIES." IT'S FILLED WITH AWFUL, UNPLEASANT THI--

KNOCK! KNOCK!

YES?

TELEGRAM FROM THE **TULSA** DAILY HERALD.

"HAVE FOUND BLOOM COUNTY FEATURE UNSATISFACTORY. AM CANCELLING IMMEDIATELY. WILL REPLACE WITH ANY STRIP **NOT** STARRING UGLY PENGUIN WITH FAT NOSE."

WELL! I... OO!...WHY YOU... OO! IT'S-MMPH!!

TOUR'S OVER!

WHO'S BEEN SHOOTIN' AT US, LUKE?!

I TELL YA, IT'S THEM CRITTERS, ABNER!

EXCUSE ME...

AFTER THE BOYS SHOOT, SKIN AND GUT THE BOTH OF YOU, WE'LL BE TYING YOU TO THE FENDER OF OUR TRUCK AND TAKING YOU HOME TO EAT. NOW THEN, HOW DO YOU PREFER TO BE PREPARED?...

NOW PERSONALLY, I'D JUST **LOVE** A COUPLE OF NICE, PLUMP, JUICY RUMP ROASTS... BUT THEN THERE'S ALWAYS STEW!

WHAT A BUNCH OF...OF... ANIMALS!!

THAT'D BE THE ROASTS THEN. FINE!

SURE WOULD LIKE TO BAG A 'COON, LUKE. OR 'POSSUM. MAYBE A WOODCHUCK. HOW 'BOUT YOU, LUKE?

ANYTHING. I WANT ANYTHING.

SAY, LUKE... IS THAT A "YELLOW-TAILED PHEASANT" OVER THERE?!

NOPE! IT'S A "RED-BELLIED SAPSUCKER"! AND THEM'S GOOD EATIN'!

BLAM!

ZING!

WHAT WAS THAT?

I DUNNO!

GOOD SHOT!

OO! WHAT WAS IT?

A "FAT-BELLIED STOGIE SUCKER"! AND THEM'S GOOD EATIN'!

31

YOU'RE WHISTLING, STEVE.

WHAT?

YOUR NOSE WAS WHISTLING WHILE YOU WERE KISSING ME.

DO YOU ALWAYS DRAW ATTENTION TO A MAN'S PHYSICAL EMBARRASSMENTS DURING TENDER MOMENTS?

STEVE, THE WHOLE BAR COULD HEAR IT.

WELL MAYBE WE SHOULD JUST OPEN DEBATE ON THE QUALITY OF MY **BREATH**, TOO!

MAYBE WE SHOULD.

TURN IT TO "THE 'A' TEAM."

CLICK... CLICK...

WHO SAID THAT?!

US! THE COCKROACHES! TURN IT TO "THE 'A' TEAM"!

FORGET IT. I'M WATCHING THE NEWS.

TURN IT TO "THE 'A' TEAM" OR WE'LL PICK ONE UNSPECI- FIED DAY THIS YEAR AND HIDE IN YOUR SCRAMBLED EGGS.

OO...I PITY DA FOOL! I PITY DA FOOL!...

YEAH! HA! HA! HA! HA! HA! GREAT!

AND NOW! THE **MTV** DRAWING TO SEE WHICH ONE OF YOU OUT THERE WINS A MAJOR ROLE IN THE NEXT TESS TURBO HIT VIDEO!...

AND...HERE IT IS! UH... LESSEE...THE PRINTING ON THE ENTRY BLANK IS EXTREMELY CRUDE...BUT...THE WINNER IS...

YEAH? YEAH?

MR. STEVE DALLAS OF BLOOM COUNTY!

YOW!

STEVE! YOU OUT THERE?! IF NOT, ONE OF YOU ROCK N' ROLLERS GO TELL HIM HE WON THE CONTEST!

YEAH! RIGHT AFTER I TELL HIM HE ENTERED!

34

...IN HONOR OF WHAT WOULD HAVE BEEN BILL THE CAT'S FOURTH BIRTHDAY, VARIOUS CHARTER MEMBERS OF THE NATIONAL BILL THE CAT FAN CLUB HAVE BEEN ASKED TO SHARE THEIR FEELINGS ON TODAY'S BITTERSWEET OCCASION:

OO...BILL HOWLED THE SONGS WHICH MAKE THE WHOLE WORLD SING...OO, BILL HOWLED THE SONGS AND SAID STUUUPID THINGS...OO, BILL HOWLED THE SONGS WHICH MAKE THE YOUNG GIRLS SICK...YES, BILL IS GROSS BUCKETS!... AND HE HOWLS THE SONGS!...

YEAH!

COOKIN' NOW!

OO! OO! OO!

HELLO. THIS IS MY OWN CAT "ELVIS SNOOGUMS." I LOVE CATS. ELVIS IS 9½. I FORCE-FEED HIM PETROLEUM JELLY FOR HIS HAIRBALLS. IF HE CROAKS, I'LL NAME THE NEW ONE "BILL SNOOGUMS."

BILL IS SIMPLY A VUNDERFUL FELLOW. A GOOD FRIEND...GOOD BACKGROUND...AND OO!... IS BUCKLEY LOADED! LOTSA DOUGH! AND I TINK DAT...UH...DAT... HUH? VHAT? VHAT'S WRONG? ISN'T ALL DIS FOR "BILL DA ARISTOCRAT?"

I LOVED BILL THE CAT. SO I MADE THIS BILL DOLL OUT OF SOME OLD CURTAINS. I THINK IT IS A GOOD LIKENESS. MOM WANTS TO BURN IT 'CAUSE IT MAKES THE DOG THROW UP.

AH YES...BILL THE CAT...GOOD OL' BILL THE CAT... GOOD OL' DUMB STUPID UGLY HAIRY SMELLY BILL THE ★◑#!! CAT...MMPHMPH!

AND SO IT STARTS AGAIN... MIDNIGHT MONSTERS AND NOCTURNAL NASTIES...ONE CAN ONLY WONDER WHAT OTHER FOLKS FIND IN THEIR LATE-NIGHT ANXIETY CLOSETS...

CREEAK...

STEVE DALLAS...ON BEHALF OF ALL YOUR PAST LOVERS...I'D LIKE YOU TO KNOW THAT WE ALL THINK THAT WHEN IT COMES TO KISSING, YOU RANK ALL THE WAY UP THERE WITH... WELL... WITH SQUID.

HA HA HA HA HA

OLIVER WENDELL JONES!... I AM THE GHOST OF SLIDE RULES PAST...COME BACK TO ME!!

AAIGH! NEVER!!

GREETINGS, MR. BLOOM. WE'RE DA COPYRIGHT LAWYERS FER UNITED FEATURE SYNDICATE. ME AND ROCCO BEEN NOTICIN' A FEW SIMILARITIES TWIXT OUR "GARFIELD" AND DAT "BILL DA CAT" JOIK... AIN'T DAT RIGHT, ROCCO?

YEAH... RIGHT...

YOU, UH... WHITE MEAT OR DARK MEAT?

SMACK

WELL, MR. BINKLEY...YOUR SON'S APTITUDE TESTS SEEM TO INDICATE THAT HE'S BEST SUITED FOR DESIGNING LADIES' EVENING WEAR. OR COLLECTING GARBAGE. EITHER ONE.

40

AN EDITORIAL REBUTTAL

The publishers of this feature welcome Professor Burton Wellsly Kingfish III, Dean of the Harvard School of Law, with his presentation of an opposing viewpoint to opinions previously and innocently expressed in this space.

I'D LIKE TO APOLOGIZE FOR MY BEHAVIOR YESTERDAY. I WAS A FOUL-MOUTHED DULLARD AND SHOULD BE DUTIFULLY *KEEL-HAULED* FOR IT.

IN HOPE OF ONCE AGAIN SITTING TOGETHER IN BROTHERHOOD, ALLOW ME TO OFFER THE FOLLOWING GESTURE AS A TOKEN OF MY AFFECTION...

SO WHAT'S A DAMP TUSH BETWEEN GOOD FRIENDS?

OO!... AH! YES... A LITTLE LOWER, MY DOVE... OO! WHAT? WHAT'S THAT, MY LITTLE BOOBOOCITOS?... WHY NO... NO, I DON'T THINK A QUICK FOOT MASSAGE WOULD HURT YOUR JOURNALISTIC CREDIBILITY, MISS SAWYER...

ZZZ

POOF!

WAS I TALKING OUT LOUD AGAIN?! WHAT'D YOU HEAR?! NAMES?... DETAILS? WHAT?! WHAT?! YOU *DID*, DIDN'T YOU?!!

OOO DARN IT! DARN IT! DARN IT!

COME ALONG, MY LITTLE BOOBOOCITOS.

BAD DAY. ROUGH DAY. NEED TO UNWIND...

SOLITUDE... QUIET... YEP... TONIGHT'S ITINERARY IS SET...

DALLAS

A COUPLE OF BREWS... A LITTLE TV...

..AND A LITTLE MOTHER.

SURPRISE, STEVIE! DINNER'S ON THE TABLE! I LET MYSELF IN THROUGH THE BACK WINDOW WITH A BRICK.

I'M SORRY, MA...I'M NOT STAYING IN TO WATCH TV WITH YOU TONIGHT. NOT TONIGHT. NO WAY. TONIGHT I GO OUT!

AND I REFUSE TO FEEL GUILTY ABOUT IT! IN FACT, I PLAN TO ACT IRRESPONSIBLE, GET DRUNK, COMMIT CRIMES AGAINST NATURE AND GET DANGEROUSLY MIXED UP WITH THE KIND OF WOMEN YOU IMAGINE ME WITH IN YOUR WORST NIGHT-MARES!

OKAY!...HERE I GO! SEE YA LATER, MA! HERE I GO!

"FAMILY FEUD" OR "TIC-TAC-DOUGH." YOU CHOOSE.

DO YOU SMELL THAT, OPUS? DO YOU SENSE WHAT'S IN THE AIR THESE DAYS?

SPRING?

NO... MORE THAN THAT... IT'S IN THE WIND... BREATHE DEEP... WHAT DO YOU SMELL?

SNORT SNORT

SNIFF!

DIRTY SOCKS.

POLITICS!

IT'S CAUCUS TIME...!!

AND SO IT WAS. INDEED, IT WAS TIME TO REIGNITE THE SLUM-BERING FIRES OF POLITICAL FERVOR AMONG THE MEADOW PARTY FAITHFUL...

I'M FERVOROUS! I'M FERVOROUS!

WAP! WAP!

...AND TO REINVIGORATE THE PREVIOUSLY NOMINATED VICE-PRESIDENTIAL CANDIDATE...

YOUR WAKE-UP CALL, MR. OPUS...

YES, IT PROMISED TO BE A TIME TO REMEMBER!

A RAUCOUS CAUCUS, AS IT WERE.

BOBBLE BOBBLE BOBBLE BOBBLE

HERE'S THE SCHEDULE OF THE SPECIAL-INTEREST GROUPS THAT OUR VICE-PRESIDENTIAL CANDIDATE WILL BE VISITING THIS WEEK. THAT'S YOU.

I AM AWARE OF THAT.

LESSEE... MONDAY IS THE "BROTHERHOOD OF STAMMERING WORM FARMERS"... TUESDAY, "BOSTONIANS FOR BUDDHA"... WEDNESDAY, "THE GAY SPELUNKERS ASSOCIATION"...

AND OF COURSE, THURSDAY IS PHYLLIS SCHLAFLY'S CIVIL RESTRICTIONS GROUP... THE "L.A.W.".

WHAT'S THAT?

"LADIES AGAINST WOMEN"

OO... SOUNDS RADICAL.

AND THUS DID THE CANDIDATE TAKE HIS SPECIAL CAMPAIGN MESSAGE TO THE PEOPLE...

THE PEOPLE

...A MESSAGE OF HOPE... OF DELIVERANCE... OF UNIVERSAL JOY:

AHEM...

NO MORE "WHERE'S THE BEEF?" JOKES!!

POUND!

AND THE PEOPLE REJOICED!

GOD BLESS YOU, BROTHER!

YES, YES... THANK YOU! HALLELUJAH!

AHEM...

THE AMERICAN MEADOW PARTY

GRBLB BLABT UNT MIPT SPEEB!! OOT PIFFOO BLABOO...

THE AMERICAN MEADOW PARTY

THE AMERICAN MEADOW PARTY

WOULD SOMEONE PLEASE GIVE THE TELEPROMPTER A SWIFT KICK...

THE AMERICAN MEADOW PARTY

MOTION CARRIED! OUR NATIONAL CONVENTION IN JULY WILL BE HELD IN SAN FRANCISCO. ANY OBJECTIONS?

SAN FRANCISCO?

AS THE SOLE REPRESENTATIVE OF THE RIGHT WING AND MORAL CONSCIENCE OF THIS PARTY, I CERTAINLY **DO** HAVE AN OBJECTION TO HAVING OUR CONVENTION IN A CITY WIDELY KNOWN TO HAVE SO MANY OF... OF...

THEM.

HILLS?

NO, NO... "**THEM**"!

"RICE-A-RONI"?

READ MY LIPS, BOY.

OKAY, MEMBERS... THE FIRST BALLOT HAS BEEN CAST AND HERE ARE THE RESULTS OF THE PRESIDENTIAL NOMINATIONS...

THE AMERICAN MEADOW

JOHN ANDERSON : 3 VOTES. ELIZABETH DOLE : 3 VOTES. G. GORDON LIDDY : 2 VOTES. STEVE DALLAS : 1 VOTE...

TAP TAP TAP

AND ONE SYMPATHY VOTE FOR ERIK ESTRADA.

HE NEEDS THE WORK.

...AND THE VOTING CONTINUED...

YAAAAAA!!

THIS IS AN EXIT POLL! HOW OLD ARE YA? ARE YA RICH OR POOR? SHORT OR TALL? SMART OR DUMB? FRESH OR STINKY? YOU EAT QUICHE? WITH OLIVES? PITTED OR NON-PITTED? WHO'D YA VOTE FOR BACK THERE?

THAT'S THE MEN'S ROOM.

RIGHT! HAND SOAP... SOLID OR LIQUID?

AND THUS THE VOTES WERE VOTED AND THE DELEGATES DELEGATED... AND, BY GOLLY, THE PRESIDENTIAL NOMINATION APPEARED ALL LOCKED UP...

OH NO... OH NO NO NO...

YES, THE PEOPLE HAD SPOKEN.. AND THEY HAD SAID...

BILL THE CAT!!

...WHICH PRESENTED THE SEASON'S FIRST POLITICAL CRISIS.

HE'S DEAD!!

YEAH, WELL, SO WAS GARY HART.

POUND!

AND NOW! AVAILABLE AT LAST! THE IBM 4000 PC SR SYSTEM... BUT NOW FEATURING TINT CONTROL!

HACKERS, AS A RULE, DO NOT HANDLE OBSOLESCENCE WELL.

OLIVER WENDELL JONES! I HAVE SOMETHING FOR YOU!

COMING, MOTHER.

HERE.

A GLOVE?

A MICHAEL JACKSON GLOVE! FOR MY OWN LITTLE MICHAEL JACKSON!

WELL. THAT'S VERY CONSIDERATE OF YOU. YES. A "MICHAEL JACKSON GLOVE," YOU SAY?

LIKE IT?

I'M IN PARADISE. WHERE'S THE OTHER ONE?

SO! I UNDERSTAND YOUR MOTHER'S BEEN WORKING ALL DAY TO TURN YOU INTO "HER OWN LITTLE MICHAEL JACKSON", EH, SON?

TRAGICALLY, IT IS TRUE.

WELL, YA LOOK TERRIFIC! BOY, SHE DIDN'T MISS A DETAIL, DID SHE? NOPE! NOT A SINGLE... UH...

SON... WHERE'Z THE REST OF YOUR EYEBROWS?

FLOATING IN THE HALL TOILET.

THAT BIG CLOUD LOOKS LIKE A FLUFFY CASTLE TO ME. WHAT'S IT LOOK LIKE TO YOU, OLIVER?

A LARGE, CUMULUS CLOUD.

OH, THAT'S GREAT. A TYPICALLY COLD, SCIENTIFIC RESPONSE. YA KNOW, IT'S THAT VERY SAME LACK OF SOUL WHICH ALLOWS BRAINY TYPES SUCH AS YOURSELF TO GROW UP AND CREATE SCIENCE WITHOUT CONSCIENCE... LIKE **THE ATOM BOMB!**

SO TURN OFF THE CALCULATOR, OLIVER, AND TURN ON THE SOUL!!

NOW, WHAT'S THAT CLOUD LOOK LIKE?

AN ATOM BOMB.

SAY, BINKLEY... WHAT'S THAT CLOUD LOOK LIKE TO YOU?

ME? OH. WELL. LESSEE... IT LOOKS LIKE... A BIG FACE. WITH A DOUBLE CHIN. AND BIG TEETH.

WHAT'S IT LOOK LIKE TO YOU?

RAIN.

PAD PAD PAD

HELLO! YES OH **YES** I'D LIKE TO TAKE ADVANTAGE OF YOUR ONCE·IN·A·LIFETIME SPECIAL TV OFFER FOR THE AMAZING RONCO COMBINATION "PLUM PITTER AND YOGURT SQUIRTER" FOR ONLY $39.98!!

IT DICES! IT SLICES! IT SHPLICES! IT PUSHES! IT MOOSHES! IT SQOOSHES! TRULY A DREAM MACHINE! DON'T FORGET THE FREE BONUS "POCKET DIAPER STEAMER!" I'LL TAKE SIX THOUSAND!! THANK YOU! GOOD-BYE!!

AWRIGHT... THAT'S IT. NO MORE LATE-NIGHT TV FOR YOU.

YES...YES, THAT'D PROBABLY BE FOR THE BEST...

I GOT SIX THOUSAND RONCO COMBINATION "PLUM PITTER AND YOGURT SQUIRTERS" FOR A MR. OPUS.

SORRY. THERE'S NO "OPUS" HERE.

YEAH DERE IS. SEZ RIGHT HERE... "MR. OPUS, 533 SUMMIT STREE—"

HE DIED. LAST WEEK. HIT BY A BLIMP.

WELL WHAT DA ★@!!# AM I S'POSED TO DO WI—-

SORRY. THANK YOU. GOOD DAY.

HE'S GONE.

OH, I AM SO EMBARRASSED!

NO WAY. WE HARDLY KNOW EACH OTHER. BUG OFF.

C'MON, PRETTY LADY... DON'T BE COY...

NO. I'M SORRY, BUT "THE SEXUAL REVOLUTION" IS OVER.

WHAT? SINCE WHEN?

I'M NOT SURE. LAST MONTH, I THINK. "TIME" MAGAZINE SAID SO.

BIG SHMEAL!

CARING... IS BACK "IN."

I CARE FOR YOU, HOT MAMA!!

NOW! QUICK! PICK UP THAT PHONE AND ORDER YOUR AMAZING "IN-THE-SKIN" TOMATO SCRAMBLER! NOW! GO!

NO. I DON'T NEED A TOMATO SCRAMBLER.

"NEED? NEED?!" YA DIDN'T NEED ABSURDLY OVER PRICED "CALVIN KLEIN JEANS".. BUT YOU ALL BOUGHT 'EM WHEN I TOLD YOU TO, DIDN'T YA??

YEAH... BUT...

WHO NEEDED "CABBAGE PATCH DOLLS"?! OR HOME COMPUTERS? OR JIMMY CARTER? NOBODY!! BUT YA BOUGHT 'EM CAUSE I TOLD YOU TO!!

ARGH!

TRULY A LEGACY OF SHAME.

THAT'S "TOMATO SCRAMBLERS." ORDER A DOZEN.

AH... THE PLUSH LEGAL OFFICES OF BLOOM COUNTY'S ONLY LAWYER...MR. STEVE DALLAS. SAY THERE, HOW'S BUSINESS?

OH IT'S JUST AWWWFUL...

NOT A SINGLE LAWSUIT IN MONTHS. CAN YOU BELIEVE IT?!

SIGH.

NOW, WHAT THIS TOWN NEEDS IS TWO LAWYERS! YEAH!

SIR! MR. DALLAS! A CLIENT! WE'VE GOT A CLIENT! WAKE UP! LET'S GO!! A CASE! A CASE! HUP! HUP!!

ZZZz

UP! UP! LET'S GET MOTIVATED!! JUSTICE! CRIME! DEFENDING THE UNDERDOG! PROTECTING THE POOR! RIGHTING THE WRONGS! YEAH! LET'S MOTIVATE!! WOO! WOO!

$ DOUGH.

UP! UP! WOO! WOO! TO THE BRIEFS, BOYS!!

HELLO, MRS. WHACKER. I'M YOUR LAWYER, STEVE DALLAS. PLEASE EXCUSE MY APPEARANCE... I'M SUFFERING FROM AN AWESOME HANGOV-- ER...HEADACHE.

VISIT HOUR 7-9 8

NOW THEN...DON'T YOU WORRY... NO ONE REALLY BELIEVES YOU AXE-MURDERED YOUR HUSBAND. LEAVE MATTERS TO ME AND I'LL GET YOU OUT OF THIS MESS. NO PROBLEM.

NOW. ARE YOU EMOTIONALLY PREPARED TO GO OVER THE DETAILS AGAIN?

I THINK SO.

WHAT WERE YOU DOING AT THE TIME OF THE ALLEGED CRIME?

ALLEGEDLY TURNING CHARLIE INTO CHOPPED LIVER! WHACKITY-WHACK!

NOW, MRS. WHACKER... YOU KNOW YOU DIDN'T MURDER YOUR HUSBAND... YOU'RE JUST UPSET... CONFUSED...

NOW YOU JUST LISTEN TO ME...

FOR TEN YEARS, CHARLIE HAD BEEN HANGING HIS DIRTY SOCKS ON THE HALL BANISTER, SPITTING ON MY GERANIUMS, AND CALLING ME "PUDGE-POT." AND LATELY HE'D BEEN FORCING ME TO WATCH "DICK CLARK'S CENSORED BLOOPERS" EVERY DAMNED FRIDAY NIGHT...

NOW I ASK YOU, MISTER DALLAS... WHAT WOULD YOU DO IF YOU WERE MARRIED TO SUCH A MAN?

WELL --

YOU'D TAKE AN AXE TO 'IM, THAT'S WHAT YOU'D DO!

AND NATURALLY YOU'D LIKE YOUR CLIENT FREED WITHOUT BAIL BECAUSE SHE ISN'T ACTUALLY A HOMICIDAL AXE MURDERER.

SHE'S A LAMB, YER HONOR.

WELL, FINE, MR. DALLAS! SHE'S RELEASED INTO YOUR CARE UNTIL THE TRIAL.

MY CARE?

SPECIFICALLY... YOUR HOUSE.

MY HOUSE?

GOOD DAY. OR RATHER, GOOD-BYE.

NOW WAIT A MINUTE...

WOOSH!

YEP. THAT'S IT. ALL THROUGH.

THE EFFICIENT LEGAL SECRETARY TO FAMED ATTORNEY STEVE DALLAS HAS FINISHED THE DAY'S WORK AND IS SETTLING INTO BOREDOM.

IT IS IDLE TIME SUCH AS THIS WHEN THE GREAT AMERICAN OFFICE WORKER KNOWS **EXACTLY** WHAT TO DO...

...XEROX VARIOUS PARTS OF ONE'S BODY WHEN NOBODY'S LOOKIN'.

EL BLOB! GET IN HERE!

COMING, YOUR LEGALNESS!

TAKE A LOOK AT WHAT I FOUND IN THE WASTEBASKET. SOMEBODY'S BEEN MESSING WITH THE XEROX MACHINE. CAN YOU MAKE OUT JUST WHAT THE HECK THIS IS A COPY OF?

WELL, LET'S SEE...

IT COULD BE A LOAF OF BREAD. OR SEVERAL POUNDS OF COOKIE DOUGH. OR A DEFLATED VOLLEYBALL. VERY DIFFICULT TO SAY, EXACTLY.

IT MIGHT ALSO BE AN **EXTREMELY** ATTRACTIVE TUCKUS.

WAKE UP! WAKE UP! TODAY'S THE DAY! HALLELUJAH, HOT PATTOOTIES! IT'S **TRIAL** DAY!!

YES, BOLDLY, THE HOT, YOUNG DEFENSE ATTORNEY PREPARES FOR THE FIRST BLOODY BATTLE... BUT **FIRST**... A DRESS REHEARSAL FOR THE OBLIGATORY PRESS CONFERENCE ON THE COURTHOUSE STEPS...

THE VIDEOTAPES ARE RIGGED! THE WITNESSES ARE CORRUPT! THE PROSECUTORS ARE NAZI DRUNKARDS AND MY CLIENT WAS FRAMED! BY THE WAY, SHE WAS BORN-AGAIN LAST TUESDAY. AND I HAVE NO FURTHER COMMENT SINCE I CERTAINLY WOULDN'T WANT TO SEE THIS CASE TRIED IN THE MEDIA.

YET ANOTHER TRIUMPHANT PERFORMANCE OF THE FAMED "DELOREAN DESPERATION DEFENSE"!

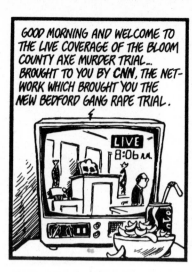

GOOD MORNING AND WELCOME TO THE LIVE COVERAGE OF THE BLOOM COUNTY AXE MURDER TRIAL... BROUGHT TO YOU BY *CNN*, THE NETWORK WHICH BROUGHT YOU THE NEW BEDFORD GANG RAPE TRIAL.

AS WE PAN ACROSS THE ROOM, WE SEE THE DEFENSE COUNSEL, APPARENTLY GOING OVER LAST MINUTE STRATEGY.

STEVE? YOO HOO!

AND HERE, OF COURSE, IS THE DEFENDANT, MRS. ALICE "ONE-STROKE" WHACKER, ACCUSED OF TURNING HER HUSBAND INTO LIVERWURST.

BILL LIVES

BUT NOW, A WORD FROM OUR SPONSOR...

GINSU CUTLERY

YOUR HONOR, BEFORE WE START THIS SHINDIG, THE DEFENSE MOVES TO HAVE ALL THE CHARGES AGAINST MY CLIENT DISMISSED. MY ASSISTANT WILL NOW CITE THE RELEVANT CASE PRECEDENT.

AHEM. "THORSON VS. LIBERACE," 1982. A 23-YEAR-OLD MAN FILES $113 MILLION PALIMONY SUIT, CLAIMING EMOTIONAL AND SEXUAL DEPRIVATION AFTER THE FAMED PIANO PLAYER FAILED IN HIS PROMISE TO... GET THIS... *ADOPT* HIM.

VERY NICE.

THANK YOU.

AND TOTALLY IRRELEVANT.

OH, BUT IT CERTAINLY IS A WONDER!

YER HONOR, THE PROSECUTION WOULD LIKE TO SUBMIT THE FOLLOWING EVIDEN—

I OBJECT!

I OBJECT TO THAT MOTION! I OBJECT TO YOUR NOSE! I OBJECT TO CRUMMY TV MINI-SERIES! I OBJECT TO THE ARMS RACE! AND I OBJECT TO CHRONIC HUNGER IN A WORLD OF PLENTY!!

I OBJECT! I OBJECT! I OBJECT! I OBJECT! BY GOLLY, I OBJECT!

BAM! BAM! BAM! BAM!

DAMN THE TORPEDOES! GO FOR THE GUSTO! BITE THE BIG ONE!... *THAT'S WHAT I ALWAYS SAY!!*

WE INTERRUPT FOR A DRAMATIC DEVELOPMENT AT THE AXE MURDER TRIAL. THE DEFENDANT HAS APPARENTLY FOUND A PLASTIC PICNIC KNIFE AND IS NOW RUNNING AMOK IN THE COURTROOM.

HERE'S JUDGE KIRBY, NO DOUBT CALMLY INSTRUCTING THE JURY NOT TO ALLOW THEMSELVES TO BE PREJUDICED BY THE PRESENT ACTIVITIES.

AND THIS APPEARS TO BE THE UNDERSIDE OF A TABLE. WE'RE GETTING REPORTS THAT THE DEFENDANT IS TRYING TO FILLET OUR CAMERAMAN...

OOPS. THAT'S IT. BACK TO ATLANTA.

...WE, THE JURY, FIND THE DEFENDANT, NOT GUILTY.

WHAT?

THAT'S RIGHT! NOT EVEN A SMIDGEN GUILTY!

ARE YOU PEOPLE ORANGUTANS? ANYBODY CAN SEE THAT WOMAN IS A MENACE!

BUT WE LADIES HAVE CERTAIN INSTINCTS.

SO DO I. SHE'S GUILTY... SHE HAS TO BE.

LOOK, YOUNGBUNS, GUILTY AXE MURDERESSES SIMPLY DON'T WEAR "GEORGIO ARMANI."

BUT THEY DO SELL MOVIE RIGHTS!!

O SOOTHING SUN, ON SUMMER WINGS... MAKES ME FORGET SO MANY THINGS!

LIKE WAR AND HATE AND BASIC BADNESS, LIKE FEAR AND PAIN AND LONELY SADNESS...

BUT MOST OF ALL FOR GOODNESS SAKES...

I FORGET MY PARKING BRAKES.

BINKLEY, I'D LIKE TO HAVE A LITTLE TALK.

MY PLEASURE.

SON, YOUR MOTHER AND I HAVE BEEN DIVORCED FOR A WHOLE YEAR NOW...FOR ME, A LONG, **LONELY** YEAR. AND NOW, LIFE MUST GO ON.

I THINK IT'S GETTING VERY CLOSE TO THE TIME WHEN SOMEONE NEW WILL BE ENTERING OUR LITTLE NEST. A NEW FACE...A NEW SMILE... A NEW LIFE TO LOVE AND HUG AND KISS.

SON, DO YOU REALIZE WHAT I'M TRYING TO SAY?

YOU'RE PREGNANT.

HELLO, MOM? THIS IS YOUR SON. I THOUGHT YOU MIGHT LIKE TO KNOW THAT, LATELY, YOUR EX-HUSBAND HAS GONE OFF THE MORAL DEEP END.

HE'S PACING AROUND LIKE A STARVING PUPPY...SAYING HE NEEDS "THE COMFORT OF A WOMAN'S CARESS.. THE WARMTH OF HER LIPS...AND THE TINGLING TOUCH OF HER FINGERTIPS."

NOW SURELY DAD WASN'T WALLOWING IN THIS SORT OF MORAL SEWER WHEN **YOU** WERE STILL HERE, WAS HE, MOM?

GRIEVOUSLY, TRAGICALLY, UNFORTUNATELY, NO.

WELL, I DIDN'T THINK-- HOW'S THAT?

SON...I...I'D LIKE TO GO OUT ON MY FIRST DATE. HOW DO YOU FEEL ABOUT THAT?

I'M NOT SURE. MORE IMPORTANTLY, HOW DO **YOU** FEEL ABOUT IT?

WELL, I THINK I'M READY. I'VE WAITED A LONG TIME. AND I **HAVE** MATURED.

THAT YOU HAVE. I RECKON MY LITTLE DIVORCÉ IS ALL GROWN UP!

THEN YOU DON'T OBJECT?

GET OUTTA HERE, COWBOY!

GOSH! THANKS, SON!

TAKE THE CAR. HERE'S A FEW BUCKS...

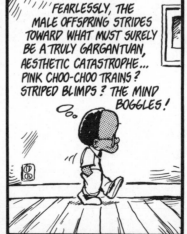

GOOD HEAVENS.

WHY DID I PUT MICHAEL JACKSON WALLPAPER ON YOUR WALL?...WELL, I'D BE HAPPY TO TELL YOU WHY...

..BECAUSE MICHAEL DOESN'T SMOKE, DRINK, TAKE DRUGS, CURSE OR FOOL WITH LOOSE WOMEN, THAT'S WHY.

DARN IT, OLIVER, YOU MIXED-UP KIDS COULD USE A GOOD, HEALTHY, ROLE MODEL, THESE DAYS!

MOTHER, THE MAN'S BEST FRIEND IS A BOA CONSTRICTOR NAMED "MUSCLES".

OLIVER WENDELL JONES? ARE YOU THERE, DEAR?

KNOCK! KNOCK!

DEAR, YOU HAVEN'T YET TOLD YOUR EASILY INSULTED MOTHER JUST HOW MUCH YOU LOVE YOUR NEW MICHAEL JACKSON WALLPAPER. DEAR?...

PRIVATE

OH, OOOOLIVERRR...?

WELL, I MUST TELL YOU THAT I AM PLEASED NOT A BIT WITH THE LOCATION OF NEXT MONTH'S MEADOW CONVEN-TION.

SAN FRAN-CISCO IS NICE IN SUMMER.

CALIFORNIA IS STOCKED WITH CRAZY PEOPLE, DEAR BOY. WOULD YOU LIKE TO KNOW WHAT THE LATEST, HONEST TO GOODNESS FAD IS OUT THERE?

NO.

WELL, I'LL TELL YA...

NOT INT'RESTED.

FIREWALKING.

HEY, I VOTED FOR DES MOINES!

ATTENTION, DELEGATES. THERE'S BEEN A BIG-SHOT INVESTIGATIVE REPORTER CALLIN' AROUND AND ASKING PERSONAL QUESTIONS ABOUT THE LATE **BILL THE CAT.**

THE MEADOW PARTY

NOW, THE LAST THING OUR DECEASED PRESIDENTIAL CANDIDATE NEEDS IS A BOOK PUBLISHED WHICH BRUTALLY EXPOSES HIS SORDID, DARK SIDE.

THUS, I DON'T EXPECT **ANY** OF YOU TO TALK TO... UH...TO... HOLD IT. —WHERE'S OPUS?

YES, THAT'S RIGHT, MR. WOODWARD... BILL WAS HEAVILY INTO SNORTING "TENDER VITTLES." WHY?

YOU WERE TELLING ALL THE UGLY, SORDID DETAILS OF **BILL THE CAT'S** SECRET LIFE TO **BOB WOODWARD,** WEREN'T YOU?

WELL, HE SEEMS LIKE A VERY NICE, INQUISITIVE, YOUNG MAN.

HE'S ALSO THE GUY WHO REGULARLY PUBLISHES THE WORLD'S MOST EMBARRASSING FACTS ABOUT FAMOUS PEOPLE LIKE OUR OWN BILL THE CAT! SO STAY AWAY FROM HIM!

SLAM!

WHERE WAS I?

UH...LESSEE... "BILL THEN PASSED OUT NUDE INTO THE GUACAMOLE SALAD..."

DRESSING FOR THE CONVENTION NEXT WEEK, EH, MR. CANDIDATE? PREPARED TO FACE THE ISSUES?

NATURALLY. I'VE ALWAYS SAID THAT ONE'S POLITICAL POSITIONS SHOULD BE AS NEAT AND TIDY AS THE KNOT IN ONE'S NECKTIE.

WHAT'S YOUR POSITION ON THE NATIONAL DEBT?

FIBULATE THE INTEREST RATES. RENOOBERATE THE MONEY MARKETS. AND PRINT MORE DOUGH.

AND NICARAGUA?

WELL, THE "CONTRAS"...FUNDED BY THE E.R.A...UH, UNDER THE AUSPICES OF GEMAYAL..ER...THE SANDINISTER...RATHER...STOP THE TERRORIST NETWORK OF GUATAMELON GORILLAS SMUGGLING EXPLOSIVE PAPAYAS INTO OHIO. PERIOD.

SOUNDS GOOD!

AND LOOKIN' SHARP!

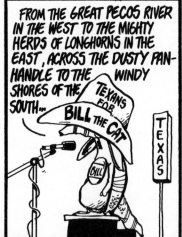

SIR...YOU'RE OUT OF ORDER. GET BACK TO YOUR SEAT.

I AIN'T QUITE SPOKEN MAH MIND, YET.

SIR...WE DON'T WANT TO HAVE TO DISCIPLINE YOU...

I AIN'T BUDGIN', YOU LITTLE SCRAP O' COW CRUD.

BACK TO YOUR SEAT!!

I'M A-STAYIN'.

MEN, LOCK THE DELEGATE FROM TEXAS INTO A BROOM CLOSET WITH SAM DONALDSON.

Y'ALL EXCUSE ME WHILE I TAKE A POWDER..

YESSIREE...AH SURE DO LOVE CONVENTIONS! ...GETTIN' AWAY FROM THE HOMESTEAD...DOIN' SOME BOOZIN' AN' FLOOZIN' WITH POLITICOS...'FACT, I WAS WITH FRITZ JUST THE OTHER DAY...

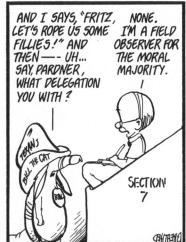

AND I SAYS, "FRITZ, LET'S ROPE US SOME FILLIES!" AND THEN—- UH... SAY, PARDNER, WHAT DELEGATION YOU WITH?

NONE. I'M A FIELD OBSERVER FOR THE MORAL MAJORITY.

ZING!

SECTION 7

NATURALLY I MEANT "ROPE US SOME FILLIES" IN THE STRICT BIBLICAL SENSE, OF COUR--

"FRITZ" WHO?

SECTION 7

OFFICIAL SMOKE-FILLED ROOM

KNOCK! KNOCK!

WHAT'S GOING ON IN THERE?

THEY'RE CONSIDERING DUMPING YOU FOR BARBARA JORDAN, WHO WOULD ATTRACT BLACKS, WOMEN AND LIBERAL INTELLECTUALS TO THE TICKET. THEY THINK **YOU** WOULD ONLY ATTRACT SHORT, FAT-NOSED PEOPLE WHO SMELL VAGUELY OF HERRING GUTS.

THE FIRST POLITICAL STUMBLE OF THE SEASON IS **ALWAYS** THE HARDEST.

SAY, OPUS...THE BARBARA JORDAN DEAL FELL THROUGH. WE'D LIKE TO KNOW IF YOU'D ACCEPT THE V.P. SPOT AGAIN.

YES! YES! THANK YOU! THANK YOU! OF COURSE! ALLOW ME TO KISS YOUR FEET! I'LL ACCEPT! I'LL ACCEPT! I'LL ACCEPT!!

POINK POINK

MAYBE.

WELL, IT'S DONE, MILO. BILL THE CAT IS OUR OFFICIAL PRESIDENTIAL CANDIDATE. AND I'VE GOT A CASE OF POST-CONVENTION DOUBTS...

I MEAN..THE PRESIDENCY! WOW! LEADER OF THE FREE WORLD! GLOBAL DESTRUCTION AT HIS FINGERTIPS! AND WE NOMINATED A DEAD CAT! A DEAD CAT!! MY GOSH..MAYBE WE SHOULD HAVE FOUND SOMEONE WITH A MORE APPROPRIATE BACKGROUND! ...A MORE EXPERIENCED BACK-GROUND...

MILO!...WE SHOULD HAVE FOUND AN AMIABLE OLD EX-"B"MOVIE ACTOR!!

DON'T BE RIDICULOUS.

OH, MILO...WE SHOULD HAVE CALLED FRED MacMURRAY...

ESTABLISHING SHOT— HOLD BRIEFLY—TRANSITIONAL SCENE

BEGIN SLOW PAN RIGHT— BRING IN MUSIC—SLOW TEMPO

MEA 198

PAN DOWN ROOM ~ DEEP FOCUS-SUSPENSE BUILDS— ZOOM IN SLOW ON FIGURE IN DOORWAY—

MEADOW 1984 VICTORY

WIDE SHOT—BRING IN STRINGS— HOLD STILL ~ BRING UP VOLUME— ROLL TIMPANI—HOLD AND ~

ACK.

Row 1:

"BILL'S DRAMATIC RETURN" —SEQUENCE #2—TRANSITION SHOT~HOLD~"AND ZOOM IN SLOW FOR IDENTIFICATION—

KEEP ZOOMING ~AUDIENCE IS BEGGING INFORMATION~ KEEP ON EDGE OF SEATS WITH VISUAL FIREWORKS —CLOSE IN~

TIGHT SHOT ~SOFT FOCUS— FAMILIAR FEATURES BECOME VISIBLE—KEEP ZOOMING TIGHTER ~"TIGHTER—

TOO MUCH!! MOOD RUINED! FACE-LIFT SCARS VISIBLE —RESHOOT

Row 2:

"BILL'S DRAMATIC RETURN" SCENE #3 ~"SPIELBERG SHOT" ~LOW ANGLE ~WIDE LENS FRONT LIT FOR EFFECT— SUBJECTS REACT TO SIGHT OF CAT~

—REVERSE SHOT—LOW + WIDE~¾ VIEW—GLYCERIN ON TONGUE FOR GLISTENING EFFECT—HOLD

REUNION ~DRAMATIC CRANE SHOT—PULL BACK + UP FOR EMOTIONAL CLIMAX —HIGHER ~"HIGHER~"

TOO HIGH!! AND TOO DAMNED SILLY! SCRATCH WHOLE EPISODE! START FRESH MONDAY

Row 3:

WELCOME BACK, SON! I'VE BEEN COOKING YOU A SURPRISE...

YOU'VE HAD WOMEN IN THE HOUSE WHILE I'VE BEEN GONE, HAVEN'T YOU, DAD?

UH-HUH! UH-HUH! I LEAVE FOR JUST **ONE** WEEK AND THE HAPPY HOME BECOMES AN UGLY NEST OF IRRESPONSIBLE DIVORCÉ BEHAVIOR...

I CAN **SMELL** THE CHEAP PERFUME...ADMIT IT... YOU'VE BEEN MESSING WITH WOMEN OF QUESTIONABLE MORAL CHARACTER.

SNIFF!

NO, I'VE BEEN MESSING WITH TARTS.

NARY A DIFFERENCE!

"THE OLD MAN HAS HAD A DAME STAYING IN THE HOUSE DURING MY ABSENCE," THOUGHT THE YOUNG AND SUSPICIOUS SON, RECENTLY BACK FROM A LONG TRIP...

"BUT THEN LET'S NOT JUMP TO CONCLUSIONS," THE BOY QUICKLY THOUGHT... PRIDING HIMSELF ON HIS BASIC FAIRNESS...

...THERE WASN'T, AFTER ALL, ANY EVIDENCE TO SUPPORT SUCH AN IDEA.

OF COURSE, HE HADN'T YET FOUND THAT CAN OF "NAIR" SITTING ON HIS TUB LOOKING REMARKABLY LIKE SHAMPOO.

NBC! THE PLACE TO BE FOR ELECTION YEAR COVERAGE...FEATURING OUR EXCLUSIVE NBC COMPUTERIZED POLL RESULTS!

HACKERS ONLY

WARDROBE

STAY OUT

HIDE THE WENCHES AND BATTEN DOWN THE ACCESS CODES...YER ABOUT TO BE BOARDED, YE SCURVY NETWORK NEWS DOGS! HAR, HAR...

Enter: "NBCNEWS"

BEEP! CLICK!

≡BEEP!≡ PASSWORD INCORRECT. ENTRY INTO NBC NEWS FILES NOT APPROVED.

Enter: "DAN RATHER IS A TURNIP."

BEEP! BEEP!

≡BEEP!≡ APPROVED.

THE DUDE IS HOT!

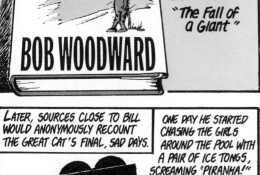

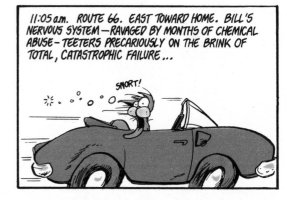

FRAZZLED

THE UGLY, SORDID LIFE, DEATH
AND REBIRTH OF BILL THE CAT

BOB WOODWARD

STILL EXCLUSIVE

The Third
and Hopefully
Final
Installment:

"He Hath
Risen Again"

IT WAS MILO BLOOM, FRIEND AND BUSINESS ASSOCIATE OF BILL THE CAT, WHO FIRST ARRIVED AT THE SCENE OF THE FIERY CAR CRASH. IT WAS ALSO HE WHO DISCOVERED THE ONLY INTACT PORTION OF THE ONCE GREAT ENTERTAINER WHICH REMAINED... HIS **TONGUE**.

HOW TOTALLY GROSS.

≥SNIFF!≤ HERE...TAKE IT, OLIVER WENDELL JONES...≥SOB!≤ I'M...I'M TOO STRICKEN WITH GRIEF...THIS IS ALL THAT'S LEFT OF BILL... PLEASE... GIVE HIM A NICE BURIAL OR SOMETHING...

OR SOMETHING.

Milo's Meat Wagon

...OR SOMETHING, INDEED! FOR THERE WERE STILL LIVING GENETIC THINGUMAJIGS AND DNA DOOHICKEYS IN THAT OL' TONGUE OF BILL'S! AND THUS BEGAN THE MOST DARING EXPERIMENT EVER TO BE CONDUCTED BEFORE BEDTIME... THE CLONING OF A CAT!

ACK!

JUNIOR Chemistry

THERE WERE, QUITE NATURALLY, SOME MINOR SETBACKS...

DRAT!

BUT THEN, SUCCESS! AND WHILE OLIVER W. JONES—SCIENTIST, HACKER AND MICHAEL JACKSON DETRACTOR—SLEPT EXHAUSTED, AN UNKNOWING WORLD MOURNED A SOUL WHO HAD FILLED THE LIVES OF MILLIONS WITH HOPE, JOY AND CAT SPITTLE...A SOUL WHO HAD ALSO...**RETURNED!**

ACK YECH BARF SNORT

SON? BINKLEY! I'M TURNING IN NOW. EVERYTHING FINE?

WELL, NO, ACTUALLY... MY CLOSET OF ANXIETIES HAS JUST DISGORGED A WHOLE GAGGLE OF GREMLINS.

THEY'RE ALL ROMPING ABOUT MY ROOM AND CAUSING A GREAT DEAL OF FUSS. WORSE, THEY ALL LOOK VAGUELY FAMILIAR. IN FACT, THERE'S A GREMLIN WHICH LOOKS FRIGHTENINGLY SIMILAR TO WALTER MONDALE AND HE'S SWATTING MY BEHIND WITH A COPY OF JIMMY CARTER'S MEMOIRS.

THAT'S WONDERFUL, SON. NONE OF IT MAKES ONE BIT OF SENSE. YOU'RE A NINCOMPOOP. NOW GO TO SLEEP.

KIDS. WHAT THEY NEED IS A GOOD DOSE OF REALITY.

PARENTS. WHAT THEY NEED IS A GOOD DOSE OF FREUD.

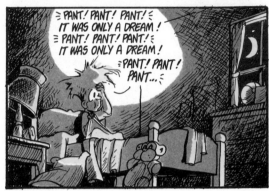

"HIGH FLIGHT"
BY JOHN GILLESPIE MAGEE, JR.

Oh, I have slipped the surly bonds of earth,
And danced the skies on laughter-silvered wings;
Sunward I've climbed, and joined the tumbling mirth
Of sun-split clouds...and done a hundred things

...You have not dreamed of...wheeled and soared
and swung
High in the sunlit silence. Hov'ring there,

I've chased the shouting wind along, and flung
My eager craft through footloose halls of air.

Up, up, the long, delirious
burning blue
I've topped the windswept
heights with easy grace
Where never lark, nor
even eagle flew.

And while with silent, lifting mind I've trod
The high untrespassed sanctity of space...

...put out my hand, and touched
the face of God.

WE INTERRUPT THIS PROGRAM FOR A SPECIAL MESSAGE FROM THE UNITED STATES FEDERAL ELECTION COMMISSION...

ON OCTOBER 28TH, THE AMERICAN MEADOW PARTY BROADCAST A PAID POLITICAL COMMERCIAL NARRATED BY THEIR V.P. CANDIDATE SHOWN HERE.

THE COMMERCIAL INCLUDED TWO PHOTO-GRAPHS APPARENTLY SHOWING RONALD REAGAN AND WALTER MONDALE IN CLOSE ASSOCIATION WITH FIDEL CASTRO AND MADALYN MURRAY O'HAIR, RESPECTIVELY.

THE COMMISSION HAS LEARNED THAT THE PHOTOS HAD BEEN TAMPERED WITH.

THE FOLLOWING ARE THE GENUINE, UN-DOCTORED PHOTOS WHICH CLEARLY SHOW WHO THE CANDIDATES WERE ACTUALLY APPEARING WITH...

"BULLWINKLE..."

AND "PUGSLEY" FROM "THE ADDAMS FAMILY".

WE HOPE THOSE RESPONSIBLE FULLY REALIZE JUST EXACTLY HOW MUCH TROUBLE THEY'RE IN.

WELCOME TO "ENTERTAINMENT TONIGHT": THIS EVENING WE PRESENT A SPECIAL INVESTIGATIVE DOCUMENTARY ..."THE UNCOUNTED HAIR: A BUSHY DECEPTION".

TONIGHT WE'LL PROVE, WITH DUBIOUS EDITING, THAT GENERAL WILLIAM WESTMORELAND'S LIBYAN BEAUTICIAN HAD SYSTEMATICALLY UNDER-COUNTED THE NUMBER OF HAIR IMPLANTS WITHIN HIS EYEBROWS.

FIB! THAT'S A DIRTY FIB!

MAYBE. HE'S ALSO A LEWDATUAL PODIATIST.

HAVE YOU NO SHAME? YOU...YOU MEDIA HAVE ALL GOTTEN JUST A TAD TOO BIG FOR YER BRITCHES!

HE'S ALSO A PERSNICUOUS LUBE-SOPPER.

LIBEL!! PPHFFT! TAKE THAT! PPPFPT!!

YAWN...

OO! WHY YOU COCKY... OO! I...OO! AARGH!!

FWUMP!!

CAREFUL... I'M REALLY GETTING ANGRY NOW...

YOU, SIR, ARE AN AMBISEXUAL WALNUT.

Challenger

"...WITH THE COSMOS DANCING BRIGHTLY ACROSS HIS VISOR, THE SPACE SHUTTLE ASTRONAUT FLOATS THOUGHTFULLY ABOVE THE EARTH...

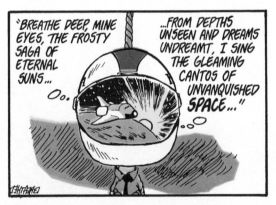
"BREATHE DEEP, MINE EYES, THE FROSTY SAGA OF ETERNAL SUNS...

...FROM DEPTHS UNSEEN AND DREAMS UNDREAMT, I SING THE GLEAMING CANTOS OF UNVANQUISHED SPACE..."

"BY THOUGHT I EMBRACE THE UNIVERSAL — WITH WINGS OF MIND I SAIL THE INFINITUDE... GLORY! 'TIS THE STARS WHICH BECKON MAN'S SPIRIT AND SET OUR SOULS ADRIFT!

Challenger

AND NOW TO WORK!... DOWN! DOWN WE REACH INTO THE CARGO BAY TO RETRIEVE OUR PAYLOAD:

...AN ANTI-SOVIET SATELLITE NUCLEAR "DEATH-BEAM" LASER.

HOW WOEFULLY UNPOETIC.

POP!

AND NOW, HERE'S ROGER MUDD WITH THE COMPUTER RESULTS FROM THE LATEST NBC NEWS POLL...

THANKS, TOM. WE ASKED AMERICANS IF THEY THOUGHT GERALDINE FERRARO WOULD ATTRACT VOTERS TO THE DEMOCRATIC TICKET. ACCORDING TO THE COMPUTER, 83% REPLIED, "BASSET HOUNDS GOT LONG EARS."

"BASSET HOUNDS GOT LONG EARS"?

RIGHT. AND THE OTHER 17% SAID, "HOLD THE PICKLES."

IT WAS ALL I COULD THINK OF.

THIS MEANS SOMETHING, ROGER.

AND NOW HERE'S ROGER MUDD WITH COMPUTER RESULTS FROM ANOTHER NBC NEWS POLL.

TOM, WE POLLED 4,000 REPUBLICANS REGARDING AUTO AIR BAG LEGISLATION. ACCORDING TO THE COMPUTER, 74% FELT THAT "OODLES OF GREEN NOODLES MAKE BLUE POODLES JUMP DER SHTROODLE."

WHAT?

THAT'S WHAT IT SAYS: 74%, NOODLES, POODLES AND SHTROODLE.

MY FINEST FREE VERSE!

DRUG HUMOR IS IN BAD TASTE, ROGER.

YOU READ IT, TOM!

PORTRAIT OF A SMALL HUMAN... A DIMINUTIVE HOUSE-APE OF THE SPECIES "BINKLEY".

PORTRAIT OF A CLOSET...CHOCK FULL OF ADOLESCENT ANXIETIES AND ASSORTED BASIC BOOGUMS...

PPHPHPT!!
YEEOW!

PORTRAIT.. OF AN ANXIETY ATTACK.

YES YOU WERE!!... YOU WERE ADOPTED FROM KURDISH YAK HERDERS!! IT'S TRUE!

NO IT ISN'T! NO IT ISN'T!!

EXCUSE US, SIR...BUT WHAT--?

SSHH! I'M KEEPING AN EYE ON ONE OF MY BIGGEST ANXIETIES.

WHICH ONE IS THAT?

THAT ONE THERE... THE ONE LURKING IN THE SHADOWS... "IMPENDING PUBERTY."

NOT A SIGHT FOR THE FAINT OF HEART NOR THE HAIRLESS OF CHEST.

THEY SAY THAT ONE'S CAPACITY FOR LOGIC AND REASON COMES FROM THE LEFT SIDE OF THE BRAIN...

AND THAT ONE'S POTENTIAL FOR EMOTIONS AND FEELINGS COME FROM THE RIGHT SIDE.

NOW, CONSIDERING MY OWN MARKEDLY LOPSIDED PERSONALITY...

..I'M SURPRISED I JUST DON'T GO FLOPPIN' OVER TO THE RIGHT FROM ALL THE WEIGHT.

SO, WHADDYA SAY WE MELT ON OVER TO MY PLACE FOR A LITTLE OF THE OL' KOOTCHIE-KOO SKIDDOO?

UH...

GREAT, BABY. BUT FIRST I'D APPRECIATE YOU SIGNING THIS PRE-AFFAIR CONTRACT.

BESIDES ABSOLVING ME OF ALL EMOTIONAL COMMITMENT, IT MAKES YOU LIABLE FOR BROKEN FURNITURE, TORN CLOTHING, ½ THE COST OF MEALS AND ALL CAR REPAIRS WHEN YOU ROAR OFF IN A JEALOUS RAGE AND WRAP MY NEW CAMARO AROUND A TELEPHONE POLE.

DOES IT MAKE ME LIABLE FOR DENTAL WORK AFTER I KICK YOUR TEETH IN?

NO, BUT NOTE THE HERPES CLAUSE, HERE...

94

THE GREAT ASTRONOMER CARL SAGAN SCANS THE HEAVENS...TAKING IN THE VASTNESS OF THE UNIVERSE...

CAN THIS ALL BE TRULY *REAL*?! BINARY SUNS! COLLIDING GALAXIES! BLACK HOLES! QUASARS! MILLIONS OF SILENT CIVILIZATIONS! INFINITY!

MY GOD, HE THINKS, COULD ANY MAN EVER TRULY GRASP THE MYSTIC AND PHILOSOPHICAL SIGNIFICANCE OF THIS REALITY WE CALL THE *COSMOS*?!?

LATER, HE WALLOWS IN THE WELCOME MUNDANITY OF A CHOCOLATE-CHIP COOKIE.

August 10th. 2:35 a.m.. Temp. 72°. With Jupiter in its final phase, Pluto's moon is visible and startlingly radiant.

..as is Mary Lou Farnheimer's. No mo—scratch that.

WANNA CATCH A FLICK? — POSSIBLY.

UH, OH. HERE'S SOMETHING RATED "PG-13". — WHAT'S "PG-13"?

"WARNING: NOBODY EVEN *NEAR* THE AGE OF 13 STARS IN THIS FILM. THIS MOVIE CONTAINS INTELLIGENT DIALOGUE, REAL-LIFE THEMES AND NOTHING THAT RESEMBLES A DARNED MUPPET."

UGLY TREND. — I DO *NOT* LIKE THIS.

BACKSTAGE IN ATLANTIC CITY... WITH THE FABULOUS "MISTER AMERICA PAGEANT" ONLY HOURS AWAY, THE EXCITED CONTESTANTS JOKE AND GIGGLE NERVOUSLY AS THEY ALL AWAIT THE CROWNING OF AMERICA'S NEW MANLY IDEAL!

"...SO THE NUN SAID, 'PASS ME THE AVOCADO!' "

HA! HA! HA! HA!

HOOT! HOOT! YOW!!

I'M JUST SO NERVOUS... SAY, WHAT'RE YOU GONNA DO FOR THE TALENT COMPETITION?

DRINK FOUR SIX-PACKS AND SING 76 VERSES OF "LOUIE, LOUIE" WITHOUT PASSING OUT ONCE.

NOT ONCE?

...OR THROWING UP.

WELL THAT BEATS MY TARGET SPITTING.

I HEAR "MISTER NEW JERSEY" IS BREAKBELCHING.

PSSST! STEVE! WATCH YER POSTURE!

WHA-? JEEZ! GET OFF THE STAGE, BLOB!

LOOK AT YOURSELF! YER LOSING POINTS IN THE SWIMSUIT COMPETITION!...FAT GUT...MINUS FOUR POINTS! ITTY-BITTY THIGH PIMPLES..SIX POINTS.

OH, BUT THEN DON'T FOR A SECOND THINK THAT I BELIEVE THESE AFFAIRS TO BE JUDGED PRIMARILY ON PHYSICAL PERFECTION... OH! HOW TACKY! HOW PERFECTLY RUDE!

BUG OFF!

DIDN'T I TELL YOU TO SHAVE YOUR BACK?! 300 POINTS!!

PSST! STEVE! SOMETHING IS ROTTEN IN DENMARK!

OR MAYBE I SHOULD SAY IT'S ROTTEN RIGHT HERE ON THIS STAGE. OVER THERE TO BE PRECISE...

...IN FACT, A CERTAIN UNNAMED CONTESTANT APPEARS TO HAVE A MORE...SHALL WE SAY...PRONOUNCED HINEY THAN NATURE ORIGINALLY PROVIDED. BUT FAR BE IT FOR ME TO SPREAD VULGAR, TACKY, NAY, MALICIOUS RUMOR.

GOOD! NOW GET--

"MISTER RHODE ISLAND" HAS STUFFED HIS SUIT!!

100

TODAY, THE GOVERNMENT-SUBSIDIZED "MINI-CAM" SLAUGHTER CONTINUES UNABATED.

ZZ... SNORT.

ENTIRE HERDS OF NEWS CREWS ARE BEING PREYED UPON AS THEY FLOUNDER HELPLESSLY, LOOKING FOR STORIES IN TRAGICALLY OVERGRAZED AREAS SUCH AS BEACHES AND PARKS...

OUR OWN REPORTER, DOT KERNS, WAS SPOTTED BY HUNTERS AS SHE WRAPPED UP A FILM REPORT ON "LULU: THE FRISBEE-CATCHING GRIZZLY" WITH THE SENTENCE, "LIFE WITHOUT LULU WOULD TRULY BE...UN*BEARABLE!*"

SHE WAS IMMEDIATELY CLUBBED AND SKINNED.

ZZ... SNORT...

H.. HELLO? ∛COUGH!∛ IS...IS ANYBODY THERE...? ∛COUGH!∛ THIS...IS...JEFF GREENBLATT... REPORTING FOR... ∛COUGH!∛ EYEWITNESS NEWS...

I'M...I'M THE LAST SURVIVOR... ∛COUGH!∛ THEY...FOUND ME FILMING A STORY ON "WHEEL-CHAIR MIMES"... ∛COUGH!∛ THEY CUT OFF MY EARS AND SET MY HAIRPIECE ON FIRE... ∛COUGH!∛

EVERYONE...ELSE... ∛COUGH!∛ GONE...DEAD...CARCASSES EVERYWHERE... ∛GAG!∛ THE...THE ONCE-MIGHTY HERDS OF MEDIA... ∛COUGH!∛ ARE WIPED OUT! EXTINCT!

THIS MORNING, "GREENPEACE" RELEASED A STATEMENT OF GENERAL APPROVAL.

GOOD EVENING. PLEASE MEET—IF YOU HAVEN'T ALREADY—MY ANXIETY CLOSET.

∛KNOCK! KNOCK!∛

...AN ENCLOSURE OF CHILDISH BEASTIES AND ASSORTED BOOGUMS...ALL OF WHICH I'VE LONG AGO LEARNED TO DEAL WITH RATIONALLY.

∛KNOCK! KNOCK!∛

WHO IIIIIIIIS IT?

JUST ME! YOUR MORTALITY!

YA'LL EXCUSE ME WHILE I CRAWL UNDER THE FLOOR-BOARDS...

CAN WE TALK?

LISTEN UP, MEADOWNIKS... TODAY WE'LL BE CONDUCTING WORKSHOPS FOR THE CANDIDATES...CONCENTRATING ON THE FOLLOWING AREAS...

"IMAGE, STYLE, APPEARANCE, SYMBOLISM, CLEVER RETORTS..."

ISSUES!

WHO SAID THAT?!

ME! I THINK AN AMERICAN ELECTION SHOULD BE ALL ABOUT ISSUES!

Blasphemer

MMPH...

MR. CANDIDATE... PLEASE EXPLAIN YOUR POSITION ON TAX INDEXING.

ACKPHFT.

THUMP!

THE ANSWER WAS FINE BUT WE CAN'T HAVE THAT SLOUCHING!

EASY... I'LL TALK TO HIM, MILO...

JUST GREAT. A FLIGHTLESS WATERFOWL AND A NEAR COMATOSE CAT. WHAT SORT OF PRESIDENTIAL IMAGES ARE THOSE?!

LOUSY, THAT'S WHAT. WE NEED A NEW, POPULAR IMAGE... HOW 'BOUT AN EX-COWBOY ACTOR?

IT'S BEEN DONE.

THEN WHAT DOES AMERICA WANT? WHAT'S IN THEIR HEADS? WHAT? WHAT? WHAT?

WHAT THIS CAMPAIGN NEEDS IS A PRIVATE SOOTHSAYER...

HEADS UP! POLLSTER-FOR-HIRE COMING THROUGH, GENTLEMEN!

TOMORROW'S ELECTION DAY... SO WHY CAN'T I FIND OUR PRESIDENTIAL CANDIDATE?

FUNNY YOU SHOULD MENTION THAT...

BILL N' OPUS
TWO FOR AMERICA

WHAT?! WHAT'S WRONG?!

NOTHING! GOOD NEWS! I THINK BILL IS GONNA SCORE BIG POINTS ON THE RELIGION ISSUE!

...HE JUST GOT ON A BUS WITH TWO HUNDRED WINOS ON THEIR WAY TO JOIN THE "BHAGWAN SHREE RAJNEESH" CULT IN OREGON.

WELL. THIS IS A POLITICAL WINDFALL.

HEY! REAGAN DOESN'T EVEN GO TO CHURCH!

ELECTION DAY. I'M A NERVOUS WRECK...THIS...? THIS IS POLITICS?..

Vote
BILL N' OPUS
FOR A WEIRDER AMERICA

...WE'RE DEAD IN THE POLLS... ANOTHER BABY PIDDLED ON MY TIE IN FRONT OF THE MEDIA... AND GEORGE WILL REFERRED TO ME AS AN "OBSEQUIOUS LIBERAL PEON".

BY GOLLY, ONE MORE LITTLE POLITICAL SETBACK AND I...I'M HEADING FOR TIMBUKTU!!

YOUR RUNNING MATE JUST RAN OFF TO BE A "RAJNEESHEE" CULTIST.

WONDERFUL. GOOD-BYE.

VICTORY

GOOD MORNING AMERICA

NEXT STOP: THE WHITE HOUSE!

DID YOU WIN?

THE EXORCISM.. HAS BEGUN.

IT'S AWFUL. I HAD TO BREAK HIM...WIPE HIS MIND BLANK AND START HIM BACK ON THAT LONG ROAD TO AMERICAN MIDDLE-CLASS VALUES.

I CAN ONLY HOPE THAT MY METHODS AREN'T TOO... SEVERE...

WARD, THE BEAVER BLEW UP THE "DAIRY QUEEN" AGAIN.

I'LL HAVE A TALK WITH HIM, DEAR.

I WONDER HOW IT'S GOING IN THERE..

DO NOT ENTER. DEPROGRAMMING SESSION →

HMM... MM...

DO NOT ENTER. DEPROGRAMMING SESSION →

.--AND NOW REPEAT AFTER ME; GARY COLEMAN IS NOT THE ANTI-CHRIST, "JELL-O" IS NOT NECESSARILY EVIL AND NO ONE HAS PROVEN THAT DOGS ARE ATHEISTS.

NEWS TO ME.

MILO! WHERE'S BILL THE CAT?

DON'T WANNA TALK ABOUT IT. THE "DEPROGRAMMING" DIDN'T WORK OUT.

DIDN'T WORK OUT? WELL, WHERE IS HE?

I SHIPPED HIM OFF.

OFF?! OFF WHERE? WHO DID YOU PASS ON OUR PROBLEM TO?! WHO?! WHO WHO WHO?!

OOF!

Betty For[d] Celebrity Rehab Cli[nic]